SOFTBALL

NAME ___________________

SEASON YEAR ___________________

TEAM NAME ___________________

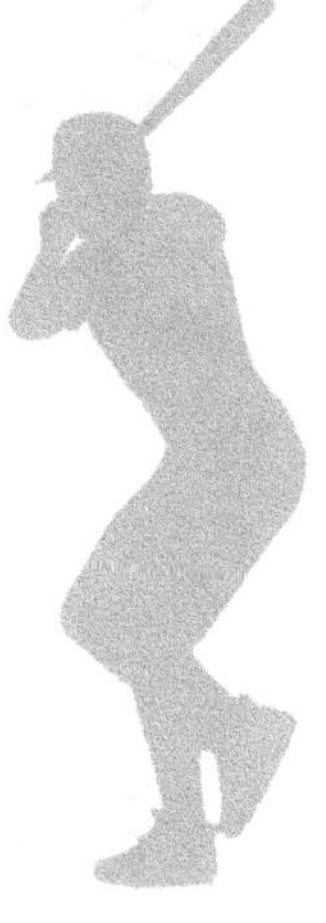

MY SOFTBALL JOURNAL

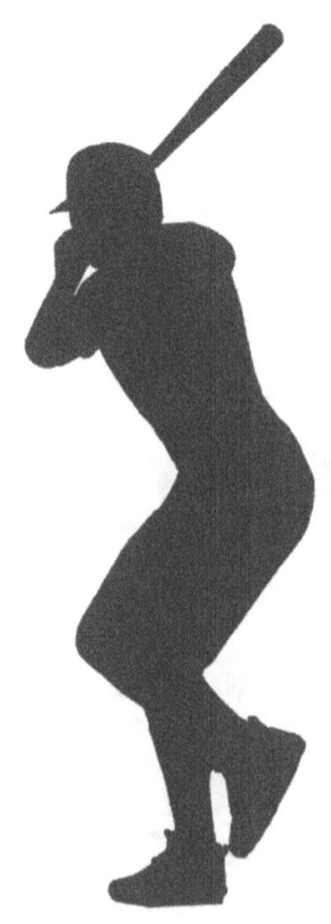

-Softball-

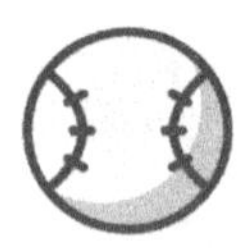

MY SOFTBALL JOURNAL

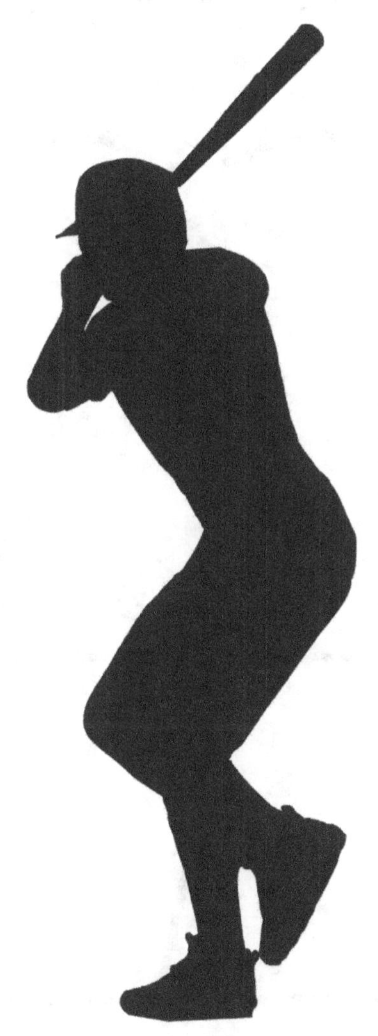

I LOVE MY

SOFTBALL

YOUR TEAM

Color in your club team or the team you support

SOFTBALL
JOURNAL
Sections

01 **Season Goals**

Write down your Top 3 Season Goals

02 **Training & Game Logbook**

Record your training sessions and game details

03 **Season Notes**

Write further details of your season to keep a record for future reference

04 **Autographs & Photos**

Gather the autographs and photos of team members, coaches and famous players

01

SEASON GOALS

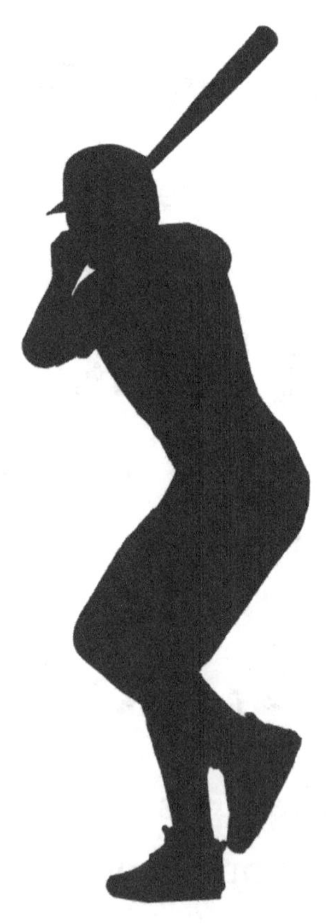

WHAT ARE GOALS AND HOW CAN THEY HELP ME?

What is a Goal?

A Goal is something that you would like to achieve. It's something that will help you improve or something that will help you remain motivated.

Goals can be 'short-term', that is, something that you would like to achieve in the next few days, weeks or months or 'long-term', being 1 year or a few years.

How can 'Goals' help me?

Establishing your goals is super important as it gives us something to strive for. When we have a goal in mind, we start to focus on those skills at training we need to improve on or encourages us listen more attentively to our coaches who can help us improve to achieve our goal.

Example: **Season Throwing Goal**: 'I will be able to throw the ball 30m accurately to base by the end of the season.'

Notice how my goal was written as '**I will be able to**...'. When setting your goals, write it out like you have already achieved the goal. This is a special secret to goal setting!

Now turn to the next page and see if you can write down 3 softball season goals. Make sure you read back over your goals each week so you keep working hard to achieve them.

01 SOFTBALL SEASON GOALS

GOAL 1

....
....
....

GOAL 2

....
....
....

GOAL 3

....
....
....

02

TRAINING & GAME LOGBOOK

TRAINING

Date:　　/　　/

Start time　　:

End time　　:

Skills Completed

Write down the skills you worked on and developed during your training sessions.

Skills to improve

Write down areas that you can improve on for your next training session

Coach & Team Focus

Write down if your coach or team has a skill or game focus you are working on

Extra Notes

Do you have additional notes or thoughts you would like to write down?

GAME DAY

Date: / /   **Start time** :

Location: ....

Home Game ⚪   **Away Game** ⚪

Game Details

.... **Vs** ....

Game Result

Our Score   Opposition Score

Coach Feedback

....

....

....

My Performance   Write down how you felt you contributed to the game. Did the coach provide you any personal feedback? Did you have any highlights? Did you have areas of improvement?

....

....

....

....

....

TRAINING

Date: / /   **Start time** :

End time :

Skills Completed

Write down the skills you worked on and developed during your training sessions.

....

....

....

....

Skills to improve

Write down areas that you can improve on for your next training session

....

....

....

....

Coach & Team Focus

Write down if your coach or team has a skill or game focus you are working on

....

....

Extra Notes

Do you have additional notes or thoughts you would like to write down?

....

....

....

GAME DAY

Date: /   /   **Start time**   :

Location: ....

Home Game   **Away Game**

Game Details

.... **Vs** ....

Game Result

Our Score   Opposition Score

Coach Feedback

....

....

....

My Performance   Write down how you felt you contributed to the game. Did the coach provide you any personal feedback? Did you have any highlights? Did you have areas of improvement?

....

....

....

....

TRAINING

Date: / /   **Start time** :

End time :

Skills Completed

Write down the skills you worked on and developed during your training sessions.

....

....

....

....

Skills to improve

Write down areas that you can improve on for your next training session

....

....

....

....

Coach & Team Focus

Write down if your coach or team has a skill or game focus you are working on

....

....

Extra Notes

Do you have additional notes or thoughts you would like to write down?

....

....

....

GAME DAY

Date: / /   **Start time** :

Location: ....

Home Game ⬤   **Away Game** ⬤

Game Details

.... **Vs** ....

Game Result

Our Score   Opposition Score

Coach Feedback

....
....
....

My Performance   Write down how you felt you contributed to the game. Did the coach provide you any personal feedback? Did you have any highlights? Did you have areas of improvement?

....
....
....
....
....

TRAINING

Date: / /   **Start time**   :

End time   :

Skills Completed

Write down the skills you worked on and developed during your training sessions.

....

....

....

....

Skills to improve

Write down areas that you can improve on for your next training session

....

....

....

....

Coach & Team Focus

Write down if your coach or team has a skill or game focus you are working on

....

....

Extra Notes

Do you have additional notes or thoughts you would like to write down?

....

....

....

GAME DAY

Date: /   /   **Start time**   :

Location: ....

Home Game ⚪   **Away Game** ⚪

Game Details

.... **Vs** ....

Game Result

Our Score   Opposition Score

Coach Feedback

....

....

....

My Performance   Write down how you felt you contributed to the game. Did the coach provide you any personal feedback? Did you have any highlights? Did you have areas of improvement?

....

....

....

....

....

TRAINING

Date: / /

Start time :

End time :

Skills Completed

Write down the skills you worked on and developed during your training sessions.

....

....

....

....

Skills to improve

Write down areas that you can improve on for your next training session

....

....

....

....

Coach & Team Focus

Write down if your coach or team has a skill or game focus you are working on

....

....

Extra Notes

Do you have additional notes or thoughts you would like to write down?

....

....

GAME DAY

Date: / /   **Start time**   :

Location: ....

Home Game ○   **Away Game** ○

Game Details

.... **Vs** ....

Game Result

Our Score   Opposition Score

Coach Feedback

....

....

....

My Performance

Write down how you felt you contributed to the game. Did the coach provide you any personal feedback? Did you have any highlights? Did you have areas of improvement?

....

....

....

....

....

TRAINING

Date: / /

Start time   :

End time   :

Skills Completed

Write down the skills you worked on and developed during your training sessions.

....

....

....

....

Skills to improve

Write down areas that you can improve on for your next training session

....

....

....

....

Coach & Team Focus

Write down if your coach or team has a skill or game focus you are working on

....

....

Extra Notes

Do you have additional notes or thoughts you would like to write down?

....

....

....

GAME DAY

Date: / /   **Start time**   :

Location: ....

Home Game ⬤   **Away Game** ⬤

Game Details

.... **Vs** ....

Game Result

Our Score   Opposition Score

Coach Feedback

....

....

....

My Performance Write down how you felt you contributed to the game. Did the coach provide you any personal feedback? Did you have any highlights? Did you have areas of improvement?

....

....

....

....

....

TRAINING

Date: / /   **Start time** :

End time :

Skills Completed
Write down the skills you worked on and developed during your training sessions.

....

....

....

....

Skills to improve
Write down areas that you can improve on for your next training session

....

....

....

....

Coach & Team Focus
Write down if your coach or team has a skill or game focus you are working on

....

....

Extra Notes
Do you have additional notes or thoughts you would like to write down?

....

....

....

GAME DAY

Date: / /   **Start time**   :

Location: ....

Home Game ⬤   **Away Game** ⬤

Game Details

.... **Vs** ....

Game Result

Our Score   Opposition Score

Coach Feedback

....
....
....

My Performance   Write down how you felt you contributed to the game. Did the coach provide you any personal feedback? Did you have any highlights? Did you have areas of improvement?

....
....
....
....
....

TRAINING

Date: / /

Start time :

End time :

Skills Completed

Write down the skills you worked on and developed during your training sessions.

....

....

....

....

Skills to improve

Write down areas that you can improve on for your next training session

....

....

....

....

Coach & Team Focus

Write down if your coach or team has a skill or game focus you are working on

....

....

Extra Notes

Do you have additional notes or thoughts you would like to write down?

....

....

....

GAME DAY

Date: / /   **Start time** :

Location: ....

Home Game   **Away Game**

Game Details

.... **Vs** ....

Game Result

Our Score   Opposition Score

Coach Feedback

....

....

....

My Performance   Write down how you felt you contributed to the game. Did the coach provide you any personal feedback? Did you have any highlights? Did you have areas of improvement?

....

....

....

....

....

TRAINING

Date: / / **Start time** :

End time :

Skills Completed

Write down the skills you worked on and developed during your training sessions.

Skills to improve

Write down areas that you can improve on for your next training session

Coach & Team Focus

Write down if your coach or team has a skill or game focus you are working on

Extra Notes

Do you have additional notes or thoughts you would like to write down?

GAME DAY

Date: / /   **Start time** :

Location: ....

Home Game   **Away Game**

Game Details

.... **Vs** ....

Game Result

Our Score   Opposition Score

Coach Feedback

....

....

....

My Performance

Write down how you felt you contributed to the game. Did the coach provide you any personal feedback? Did you have any highlights? Did you have areas of improvement?

....

....

....

....

....

TRAINING

Date: / /

Start time :

End time :

Skills Completed

Write down the skills you worked on and developed during your training sessions.

....

....

....

....

Skills to improve

Write down areas that you can improve on for your next training session

....

....

....

....

Coach & Team Focus

Write down if your coach or team has a skill or game focus you are working on

....

....

Extra Notes

Do you have additional notes or thoughts you would like to write down?

....

....

....

GAME DAY 

Date: /   /   **Start time**   :

Location: ....

Home Game   **Away Game**

Game Details

.... **Vs** ....

Game Result

Our Score   Opposition Score

Coach Feedback

....

....

....

My Performance   Write down how you felt you contributed to the game. Did the coach provide you any personal feedback? Did you have any highlights? Did you have areas of improvement?

....

....

....

....

....

TRAINING

Date: / /

Start time :

End time :

Skills Completed

Write down the skills you worked on and developed during your training sessions.

....

....

....

....

Skills to improve

Write down areas that you can improve on for your next training session

....

....

....

....

Coach & Team Focus

Write down if your coach or team has a skill or game focus you are working on

....

....

Extra Notes

Do you have additional notes or thoughts you would like to write down?

....

....

GAME DAY

Date: /   /   **Start time**   :

Location: ....

Home Game   **Away Game**

Game Details

.... **Vs** ....

Game Result

Our Score   Opposition Score

Coach Feedback

....

....

....

My Performance   Write down how you felt you contributed to the game. Did the coach provide you any personal feedback? Did you have any highlights? Did you have areas of improvement?

....

....

....

....

....

TRAINING

Date: / /

Start time :

End time :

Skills Completed

Write down the skills you worked on and developed during your training sessions.

....

....

....

....

Skills to improve

Write down areas that you can improve on for your next training session

....

....

....

....

Coach & Team Focus

Write down if your coach or team has a skill or game focus you are working on

....

....

Extra Notes

Do you have additional notes or thoughts you would like to write down?

....

....

GAME DAY

Date: / /   **Start time** :

Location: ....

Home Game   **Away Game**

Game Details

.... **Vs** ....

Game Result

Our Score   Opposition Score

Coach Feedback

....
....
....

My Performance   Write down how you felt you contributed to the game. Did the coach provide you any personal feedback? Did you have any highlights? Did you have areas of improvement?

....
....
....
....
....

TRAINING

Date: / /   **Start time**   :

End time   :

Skills Completed

Write down the skills you worked on and developed during your training sessions.

....

....

....

....

Skills to improve

Write down areas that you can improve on for your next training session

....

....

....

....

Coach & Team Focus

Write down if your coach or team has a skill or game focus you are working on

....

....

Extra Notes

Do you have additional notes or thoughts you would like to write down?

....

....

....

GAME DAY

Date: / /   **Start time**   :

Location: ....

Home Game ⬤   **Away Game** ⬤

Game Details

.... **Vs** ....

Game Result

Our Score   Opposition Score

Coach Feedback

....
....
....

My Performance Write down how you felt you contributed to the game. Did the coach provide you any personal feedback? Did you have any highlights? Did you have areas of improvement?

....
....
....
....
....

TRAINING

Date: / /

Start time :

End time :

Skills Completed

Write down the skills you worked on and developed during your training sessions.

....

....

....

....

Skills to improve

Write down areas that you can improve on for your next training session

....

....

....

Coach & Team Focus

Write down if your coach or team has a skill or game focus you are working on

....

....

Extra Notes

Do you have additional notes or thoughts you would like to write down?

....

....

....

GAME DAY 

Date: /   /   **Start time**   :

Location: ....

Home Game   **Away Game**

Game Details

.... **Vs** ....

Game Result

Our Score   Opposition Score

Coach Feedback

....
....
....

My Performance Write down how you felt you contributed to the game. Did the coach provide you any personal feedback? Did you have any highlights? Did you have areas of improvement?

....
....
....
....
....
....

TRAINING

Date: / /   **Start time** :

End time :

Skills Completed

Write down the skills you worked on and developed during your training sessions.

Skills to improve

Write down areas that you can improve on for your next training session

Coach & Team Focus

Write down if your coach or team has a skill or game focus you are working on

Extra Notes

Do you have additional notes or thoughts you would like to write down?

GAME DAY

Date: / / **Start time** :

Location: ....

Home Game ⬤ **Away Game** ⬤

Game Details

.... **Vs** ....

Game Result

Our Score   Opposition Score

Coach Feedback

....

....

....

My Performance   Write down how you felt you contributed to the game. Did the coach provide you any personal feedback? Did you have any highlights? Did you have areas of improvement?

....

....

....

....

....

TRAINING

Date: / /   **Start time** :

End time :

Skills Completed

Write down the skills you worked on and developed during your training sessions.

....

....

....

....

Skills to improve

Write down areas that you can improve on for your next training session

....

....

....

Coach & Team Focus

Write down if your coach or team has a skill or game focus you are working on

....

....

Extra Notes

Do you have additional notes or thoughts you would like to write down?

....

....

....

GAME DAY

Date: /   /   **Start time**   :

Location: ....

Home Game   **Away Game**

Game Details

.... **Vs** ....

Game Result

Our Score   Opposition Score

Coach Feedback

....

....

....

My Performance   Write down how you felt you contributed to the game. Did the coach provide you any personal feedback? Did you have any highlights? Did you have areas of improvement?

....

....

....

....

....

TRAINING

Date: / /   **Start time** :

End time :

Skills Completed

Write down the skills you worked on and developed during your training sessions.

....

....

....

....

Skills to improve

Write down areas that you can improve on for your next training session

....

....

....

Coach & Team Focus

Write down if your coach or team has a skill or game focus you are working on

....

....

Extra Notes

Do you have additional notes or thoughts you would like to write down?

....

....

GAME DAY

Date: /   /   **Start time**   :

Location: ....

Home Game   **Away Game**

Game Details

.... **Vs** ....

Game Result

Our Score   Opposition Score

Coach Feedback

....

....

....

My Performance   Write down how you felt you contributed to the game. Did the coach provide you any personal feedback? Did you have any highlights? Did you have areas of improvement?

....

....

....

....

....

TRAINING

Date: / / **Start time** :

End time :

Skills Completed

Write down the skills you worked on and developed during your training sessions.

....

....

....

....

Skills to improve

Write down areas that you can improve on for your next training session

....

....

....

....

Coach & Team Focus

Write down if your coach or team has a skill or game focus you are working on

....

....

Extra Notes

Do you have additional notes or thoughts you would like to write down?

....

....

....

GAME DAY 

Date: / /   **Start time**   :

Location: ....

Home Game ○   **Away Game** ○

Game Details

.... **Vs** ....

Game Result

Our Score   Opposition Score

Coach Feedback

....

....

....

My Performance   Write down how you felt you contributed to the game. Did the coach provide you any personal feedback? Did you have any highlights? Did you have areas of improvement?

....

....

....

....

....

03

SEASON NOTES

NOTES

NOTES

NOTES

04

Autographs & Photos

Autographs & Photo's

TRAINING

Date: /   /   **Start time**   :

End time   :

Skills Completed

Write down the skills you worked on and developed during your training sessions.

....

....

....

....

Skills to improve

Write down areas that you can improve on for your next training session

....

....

....

....

Coach & Team Focus

Write down if your coach or team has a skill or game focus you are working on

....

....

Extra Notes

Do you have additional notes or thoughts you would like to write down?

....

....

....

GAME DAY

Date: / /   **Start time**   :

Location: ....

Home Game   **Away Game**

Game Details

.... **Vs** ....

Game Result

Our Score   Opposition Score

Coach Feedback

....
....
....

My Performance   Write down how you felt you contributed to the game. Did the coach provide you any personal feedback? Did you have any highlights? Did you have areas of improvement?

....
....
....
....
....

TRAINING

Date: / /   **Start time** :

End time :

Skills Completed

Write down the skills you worked on and developed during your training sessions.

....

....

....

....

Skills to improve

Write down areas that you can improve on for your next training session

....

....

....

....

Coach & Team Focus

Write down if your coach or team has a skill or game focus you are working on

....

....

Extra Notes

Do you have additional notes or thoughts you would like to write down?

....

....

....

GAME DAY

Date: / /   **Start time** :

Location: ....

Home Game   **Away Game**

Game Details

.... **Vs** ....

Game Result

Our Score   Opposition Score

Coach Feedback

....

....

....

My Performance Write down how you felt you contributed to the game. Did the coach provide you any personal feedback? Did you have any highlights? Did you have areas of improvement?

....

....

....

....

....

TRAINING

Date: / / **Start time** :

End time :

Skills Completed

Write down the skills you worked on and developed during your training sessions.

....

....

....

....

Skills to improve

Write down areas that you can improve on for your next training session

....

....

....

Coach & Team Focus

Write down if your coach or team has a skill or game focus you are working on

....

....

Extra Notes

Do you have additional notes or thoughts you would like to write down?

....

....

....

GAME DAY

Date: / /   **Start time**   :

Location: ....

Home Game   **Away Game**

Game Details

.... **Vs** ....

Game Result

Our Score   Opposition Score

Coach Feedback

....

....

....

My Performance   Write down how you felt you contributed to the game. Did the coach provide you any personal feedback? Did you have any highlights? Did you have areas of improvement?

....

....

....

....

....

TRAINING

Date: / /   **Start time** :

End time :

Skills Completed

Write down the skills you worked on and developed during your training sessions.

....

....

....

....

Skills to improve

Write down areas that you can improve on for your next training session

....

....

....

....

Coach & Team Focus

Write down if your coach or team has a skill or game focus you are working on

....

....

Extra Notes

Do you have additional notes or thoughts you would like to write down?

....

....

....

GAME DAY

Date: / /   **Start time** :

Location: ....

Home Game   **Away Game**

Game Details

.... **Vs** ....

Game Result

Our Score   Opposition Score

Coach Feedback

....
....
....

My Performance   Write down how you felt you contributed to the game. Did the coach provide you any personal feedback? Did you have any highlights? Did you have areas of improvement?

....
....
....
....

TRAINING

Date: / /

Start time :

End time :

Skills Completed

Write down the skills you worked on and developed during your training sessions.

....

....

....

....

Skills to improve

Write down areas that you can improve on for your next training session

....

....

....

....

Coach & Team Focus

Write down if your coach or team has a skill or game focus you are working on

....

....

Extra Notes

Do you have additional notes or thoughts you would like to write down?

....

....

GAME DAY

Date: / /   **Start time**   :

Location: ....

Home Game   **Away Game**

Game Details

.... **Vs** ....

Game Result

Our Score   Opposition Score

Coach Feedback

....

....

....

My Performance   Write down how you felt you contributed to the game. Did the coach provide you any personal feedback? Did you have any highlights? Did you have areas of improvement?

....

....

....

....

....

TRAINING

Date: / /   **Start time** :

End time :

Skills Completed

Write down the skills you worked on and developed during your training sessions.

....

....

....

....

Skills to improve

Write down areas that you can improve on for your next training session

....

....

....

Coach & Team Focus

Write down if your coach or team has a skill or game focus you are working on

....

....

Extra Notes

Do you have additional notes or thoughts you would like to write down?

....

....

....

GAME DAY

Date: /   /   **Start time**   :

Location: ....

Home Game   **Away Game**

Game Details

.... **Vs** ....

Game Result

Our Score   Opposition Score

Coach Feedback

....

....

....

My Performance

Write down how you felt you contributed to the game. Did the coach provide you any personal feedback? Did you have any highlights? Did you have areas of improvement?

....

....

....

....

....

TRAINING

Date: / /   **Start time**   :

End time   :

Skills Completed

Write down the skills you worked on and developed during your training sessions.

....

....

....

....

Skills to improve

Write down areas that you can improve on for your next training session

....

....

....

Coach & Team Focus

Write down if your coach or team has a skill or game focus you are working on

....

....

Extra Notes

Do you have additional notes or thoughts you would like to write down?

....

....

....

GAME DAY

Date: /   /   **Start time**   :

Location: ....

Home Game   **Away Game**

Game Details

.... **Vs** ....

Game Result

Our Score   Opposition Score

Coach Feedback

....

....

....

My Performance   Write down how you felt you contributed to the game. Did the coach provide you any personal feedback? Did you have any highlights? Did you have areas of improvement?

....

....

....

....

....

TRAINING

Date: / /   **Start time** :

End time :

Skills Completed

Write down the skills you worked on and developed during your training sessions.

....

....

....

....

Skills to improve

Write down areas that you can improve on for your next training session

....

....

....

Coach & Team Focus

Write down if your coach or team has a skill or game focus you are working on

....

....

Extra Notes

Do you have additional notes or thoughts you would like to write down?

....

....

GAME DAY

Date: / /   **Start time**   :

Location: ....

Home Game   **Away Game**

Game Details

.... **Vs** ....

Game Result

Our Score   Opposition Score

Coach Feedback

....

....

....

My Performance   Write down how you felt you contributed to the game. Did the coach provide you any personal feedback? Did you have any highlights? Did you have areas of improvement?

....

....

....

....

....

TRAINING

Date: / /

Start time :

End time :

Skills Completed

Write down the skills you worked on and developed during your training sessions.

Skills to improve

Write down areas that you can improve on for your next training session

Coach & Team Focus

Write down if your coach or team has a skill or game focus you are working on

Extra Notes

Do you have additional notes or thoughts you would like to write down?

GAME DAY

Date: / /   **Start time** :

Location: ....

Home Game   **Away Game**

Game Details

.... **Vs** ....

Game Result

Our Score   Opposition Score

Coach Feedback

....
....
....

My Performance   Write down how you felt you contributed to the game. Did the coach provide you any personal feedback? Did you have any highlights? Did you have areas of improvement?

....
....
....
....
....

TRAINING

Date: / /   **Start time** :

End time :

Skills Completed

Write down the skills you worked on and developed during your training sessions.

....

....

....

....

Skills to improve

Write down areas that you can improve on for your next training session

....

....

....

....

Coach & Team Focus

Write down if your coach or team has a skill or game focus you are working on

....

....

Extra Notes

Do you have additional notes or thoughts you would like to write down?

....

....

GAME DAY

Date: /   /   **Start time**   :

Location: ....

Home Game   **Away Game**

Game Details

.... **Vs** ....

Game Result

Our Score   Opposition Score

Coach Feedback

....

....

....

My Performance Write down how you felt you contributed to the game. Did the coach provide you any personal feedback? Did you have any highlights? Did you have areas of improvement?

....

....

....

....

....

TRAINING

Date: / /   **Start time** :

End time :

Skills Completed
Write down the skills you worked on and developed during your training sessions.

Skills to improve
Write down areas that you can improve on for your next training session

Coach & Team Focus
Write down if your coach or team has a skill or game focus you are working on

Extra Notes Do you have additional notes or thoughts you would like to write down?

GAME DAY

Date: /   /   **Start time**   :

Location: ....

Home Game ⬤   **Away Game** ⬤

Game Details

.... **Vs** ....

Game Result

Our Score   Opposition Score

Coach Feedback

....

....

....

My Performance   Write down how you felt you contributed to the game. Did the coach provide you any personal feedback? Did you have any highlights? Did you have areas of improvement?

....

....

....

....

....

TRAINING

Date: / /   **Start time**   :

End time   :

Skills Completed
Write down the skills you worked on and developed during your training sessions.

....

....

....

....

Skills to improve
Write down areas that you can improve on for your next training session

....

....

....

Coach & Team Focus
Write down if your coach or team has a skill or game focus you are working on

....

....

Extra Notes
Do you have additional notes or thoughts you would like to write down?

....

....

....

GAME DAY

Date: /   /   **Start time**   :

Location: ....

Home Game   **Away Game**

Game Details

.... **Vs** ....

Game Result

Our Score   Opposition Score

Coach Feedback

....

....

....

My Performance   Write down how you felt you contributed to the game. Did the coach provide you any personal feedback? Did you have any highlights? Did you have areas of improvement?

....

....

....

....

....

Autographs & Photo's

Autographs & Photo's

Autographs & Photo's

Autographs & Photo's

Autographs & Photo's

Autographs & Photo's

Autographs & Photo's

SOFTBALL

Journal

-Softball-